Welcome to the Circus

PATRICE SHERMAN

TABLE OF CONTENTS

PIONEER VALLEY EDUCATIONAL PRESS, INC

FINAL BOWS

On May 14, 1917, a crowd of 30,000 people gathered at the showgrounds in Washington, DC, to watch as giant tents were set up to house 1,000 wild animals, 735 horses, 41 elephants, and all the circus performers. That night there was an audience of almost 10,000 people who paid for seats to watch the circus that was called "The Greatest Show on Earth."

Nearly 100 years later, "The Greatest Show on Earth" had its final performance. Was this to be the end of the circus?

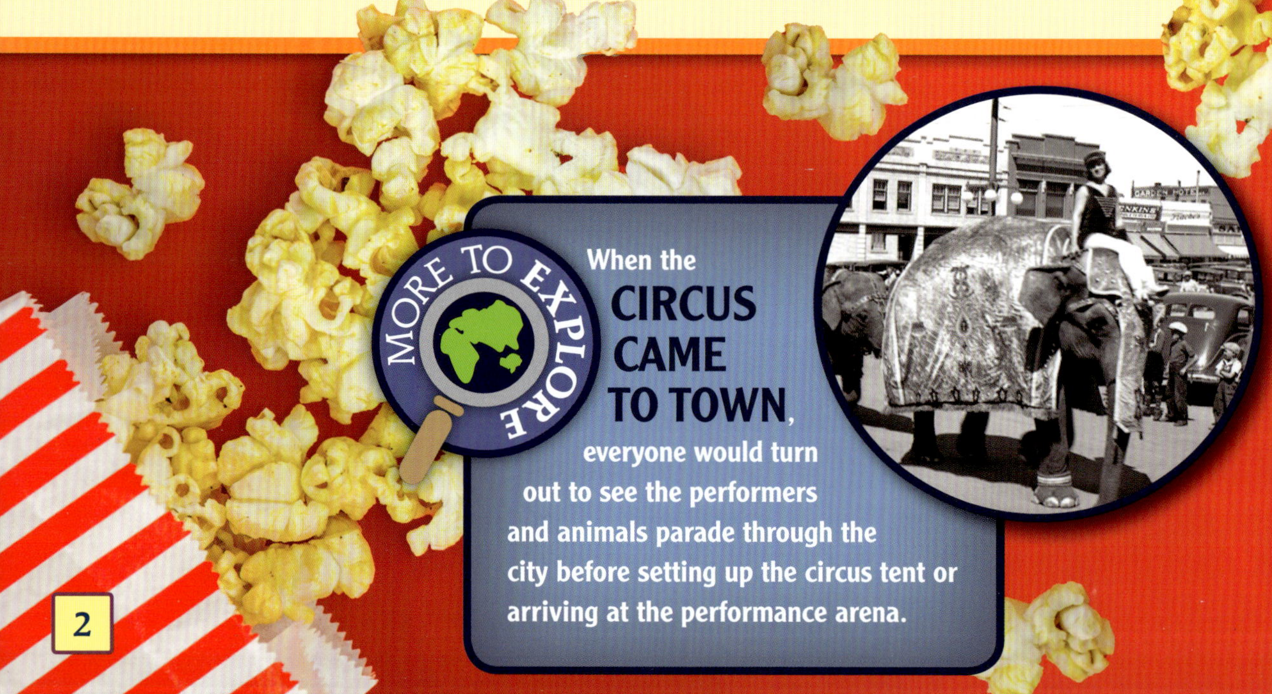

When the **CIRCUS CAME TO TOWN**, everyone would turn out to see the performers and animals parade through the city before setting up the circus tent or arriving at the performance arena.

For almost 100 years, Ringling Bros. and Barnum & Bailey was the largest, most famous US circus.

THE EARLY CIRCUS

Circuses go back to the days of **ancient** Rome. Romans held chariot races in a big arena they called a circus. Drivers raced in small two-wheeled chariots, each pulled by a team of horses. The races attracted huge crowds, where people would cheer for their favorite drivers.

Romans held chariot races in arenas they called circuses.

During the Middle Ages, **acrobats**, jugglers, and magicians entertained people at fairs and festivals. They traveled from place to place in a **troupe**, or group. Sometimes they brought trained animals like dancing bears. Most people at that time had few opportunities to travel beyond their home villages, so these entertainers were unusual and therefore exciting.

Medieval fairs had jugglers, dancing bears, and acrobats.

The first modern circus started in London in 1768. Philip Astley, a horseback riding teacher, discovered how to balance on a horse's back when it galloped in a circle. He then hired a group of trick riders to perform in his riding arena. Philip later added jugglers and acrobats to his act. People flocked to Philip's show, and the circus was born!

MORE TO EXPLORE

Philip Astley performed in a **CIRCULAR ARENA** with his small horse, which was trained to add and subtract numbers (or pretend to do so) and could also fake its own death, fire a pistol, and perform "mind-reading" tricks.

In 1793, John Bill Ricketts started the first American circus in Philadelphia, where he built a 42-foot-wide circus ring. George Washington attended at least one performance. **Legend** has it that he liked the show so much that he gave John a white horse he had ridden during the Revolutionary War.

Women have always played a starring role in the circus.

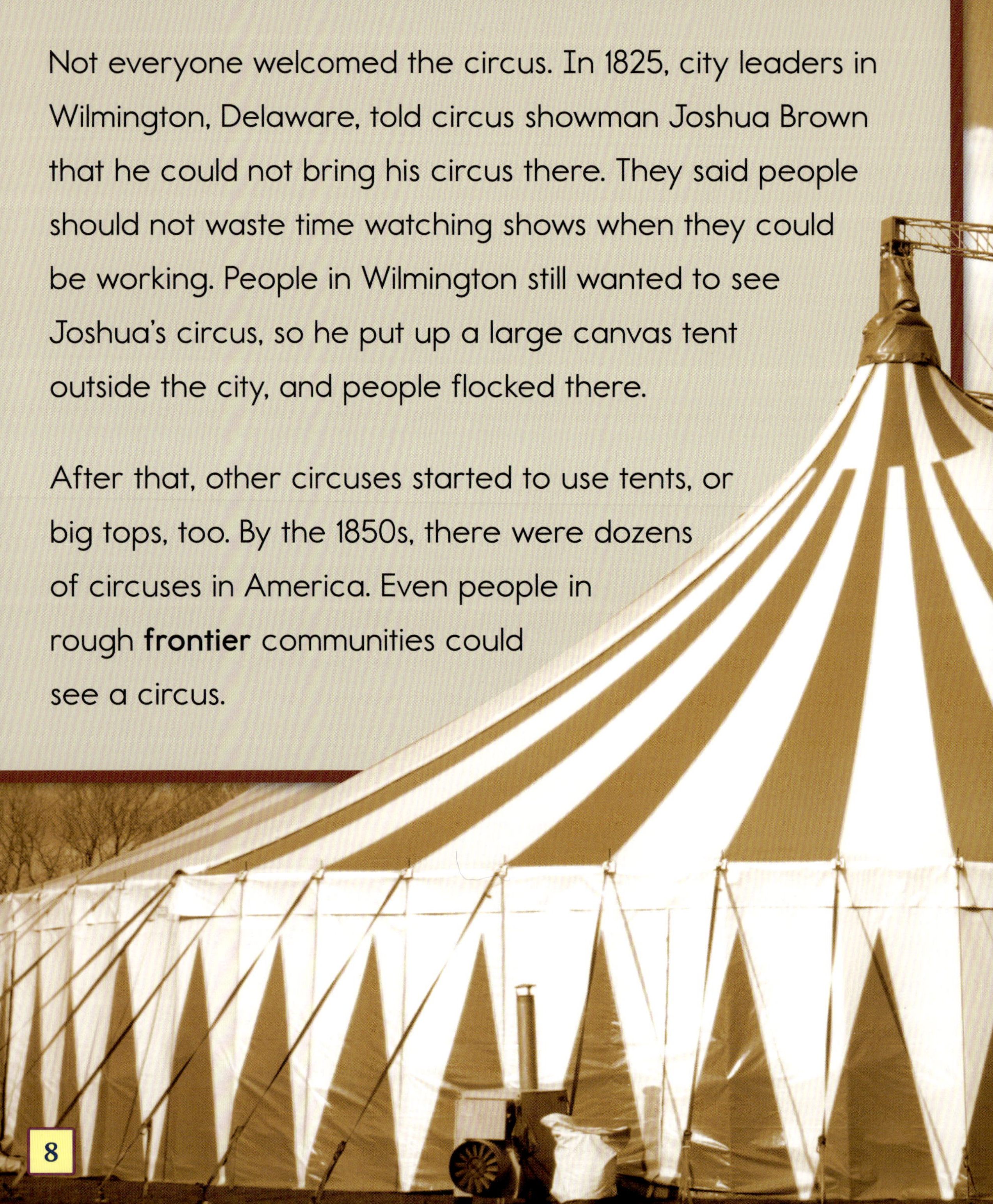

Not everyone welcomed the circus. In 1825, city leaders in Wilmington, Delaware, told circus showman Joshua Brown that he could not bring his circus there. They said people should not waste time watching shows when they could be working. People in Wilmington still wanted to see Joshua's circus, so he put up a large canvas tent outside the city, and people flocked there.

After that, other circuses started to use tents, or big tops, too. By the 1850s, there were dozens of circuses in America. Even people in rough **frontier** communities could see a circus.

Isaac van Amburgh was the first American performer to work with BIG CATS. He thrilled onlookers when he put his head in the mouth of a lion.

THE GREAT AMERICAN CIRCUS

Born in 1810, Phineas T. Barnum became the greatest circus producer in American history. P. T. believed in something he called "humbug." Humbug, he said, meant fooling people while keeping them so entertained that they didn't mind being fooled.

For instance, he told people he had a real mermaid, which turned out to be the head of a monkey sewn to the body of a dried fish. Even though many knew it was a hoax, people still paid money to come and see P. T.'s mermaid. P. T. realized people wanted to be entertained, and he was happy to please them.

P. T. Barnum's Feejee Mermaid attracted many viewers.

The main attraction of P. T.'s circus was his elephants. They were so popular that in 1884, soon after the Brooklyn Bridge was completed, P. T. paraded 21 elephants and 17 camels across the bridge to demonstrate to the community how safe it was.

In the 1880s, P. T. joined forces with James Bailey to create Barnum & Bailey. Their circus had over 1,000 performers, and it took 85 railroad cars to transport the entire circus from one location to the next. Then, in 1907, Barnum & Bailey was bought by the Ringling brothers, and in 1919, they combined the shows to create the Ringling Bros. and Barnum & Bailey Circus.

CIRCUS SUPERSTARS

Many circus performers became superstars, even some that were not human. Jumbo the elephant was one of the greatest circus stars of all time. Jumbo stood nearly 11 feet tall and weighed over five tons. Thousands came to see him at Barnum & Bailey Circus when he arrived in 1882. Unfortunately, Jumbo died in a railroad accident a few years later.

This life-size sculpture of Jumbo is displayed at Tufts University.

Other performers made a name for themselves across the world. The Flying Wallendas joined Ringling Bros. and Barnum & Bailey in 1928. A German family with a long history as high-wire artists, they were famous for their human pyramid. Antoinette Concello, a trapeze artist, was the first woman to successfully complete a triple somersault in the air and became known as the "greatest woman flyer of all time."

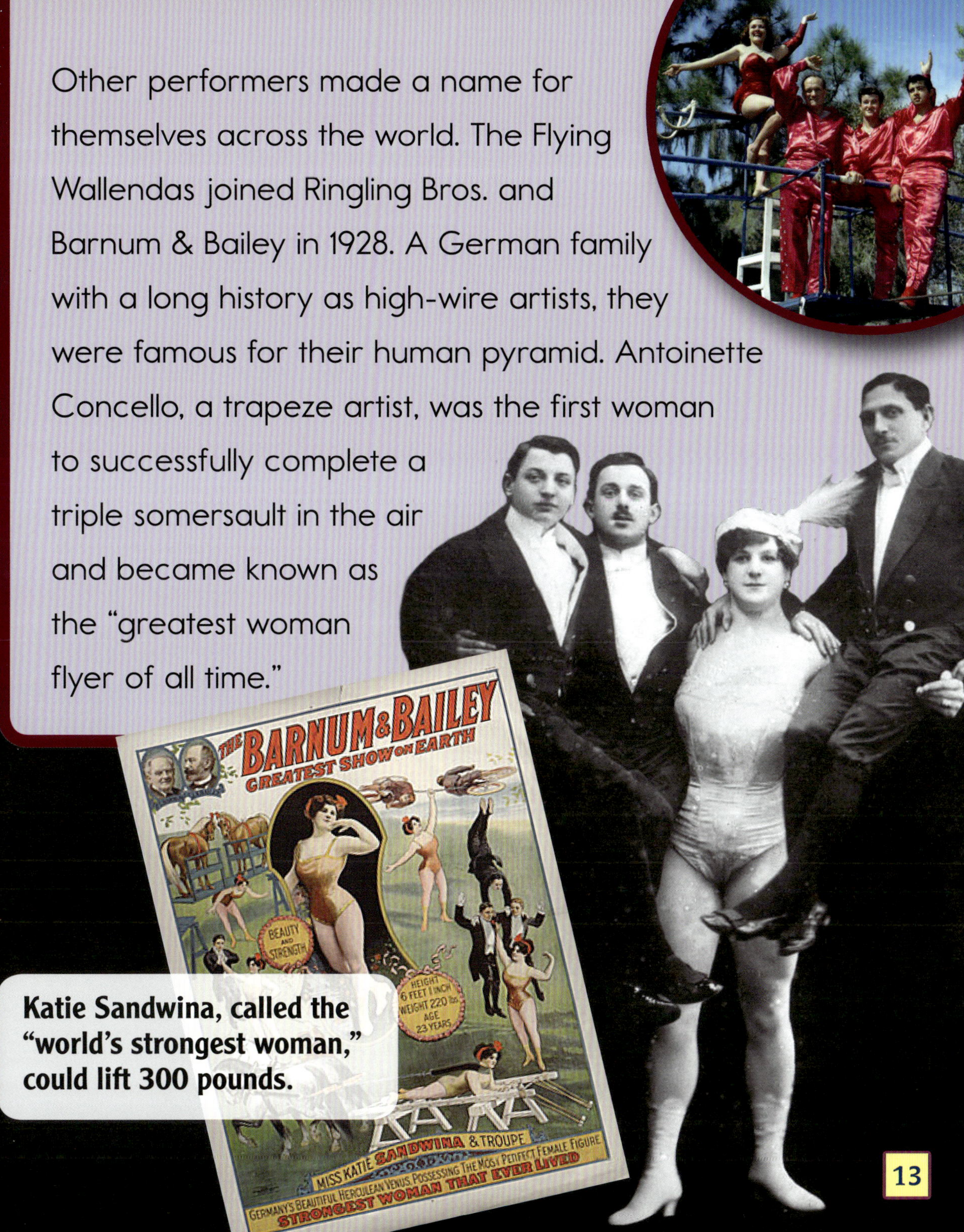

Katie Sandwina, called the "world's strongest woman," could lift 300 pounds.

THE CIRCUS CHANGES

So many people, especially children, gathered to see the circus over the years that it became an American tradition. But in recent years, many people became concerned about the well-being of circus animals. When not performing, circus animals often lived in small cages. Some trainers cared about their animals and tried to make their lives easier, but at times this was difficult because circuses had limited resources. So sometimes performing animals did not get proper treatment when they were ill. Animals like elephants could become very sad and even sick if they were separated from their own kind.

The tricks the animals learned often came from long hours of training, and many animals were punished harshly when they failed to follow the directions of the trainer. A lot of training was needed because, in the wild, bears never balance on balls, tigers don't jump through hoops of fire, and elephants never, ever ride bicycles.

Animal rights activists

have been concerned about some of the ways animals have been coerced into performing.

CHAINS were used to prevent escape when elephants weren't performing. Some elephants were chained for up to 23 hours a day.

STARVATION was a "training" technique that involved depriving animals of food and water and only providing these when the trick had been accomplished.

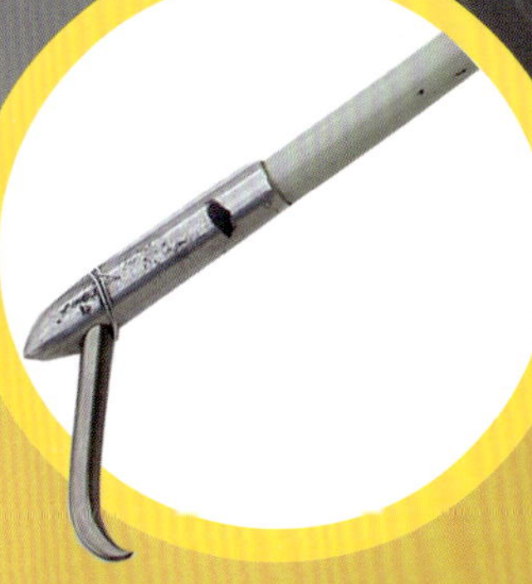

BULLHOOKS had a sharp hook at the end of a long pole that was used to dig into elephants' sensitive flesh, which could cause extreme pain.

WHIPS were used to make big cats, bears, and other animals perform.

ELECTRIC PRODS were used to teach animals to perform tricks by way of fear and pain.

By 2017, many nations all over the world and several US states had banned wild-animal acts. The trained circus animals could not be returned to the wild, so circus owners found homes for them in animal **sanctuaries**, where they could be cared for and protected.

Without the **exotic** animals to watch, attendance at the circus dropped. And the big circuses had other problems too. Many cities and towns no longer had arenas available for big circuses. Audiences began to shrink as people turned toward other forms of entertainment. On May 21, 2017, the Ringling Bros. and Barnum & Bailey Circus gave its last performance in Uniondale, New York. "The Greatest Show on Earth" was over.

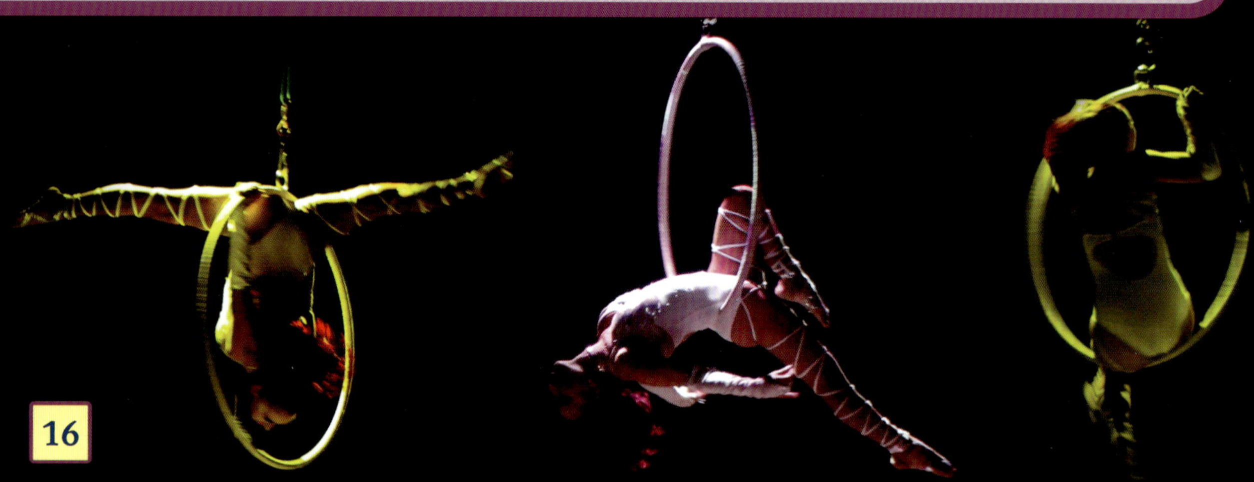

Or was it?

Although traditional circuses were gone, other types of circuses blossomed. For example, in the 1980s a new kind of circus was started in Canada. This circus had no animals, only human performers, and was called Cirque du Soleil, or Circus of the Sun. The show became a hit and continues to be popular to this day. Cirque du Soleil now performs all over the world.

The Big Apple Circus, founded in 1977, performs without wild animals.

These modern circuses have inspired a new generation of circus artists. At youth circus camps, children and teens learn **acrobatics**, tightrope walking, stilt walking, plate spinning, trapeze flying, unicycle riding, and other acts. Youth circuses give kids an opportunity to show their skills to an audience. There are more and more youth circuses and circus training schools starting across the globe.

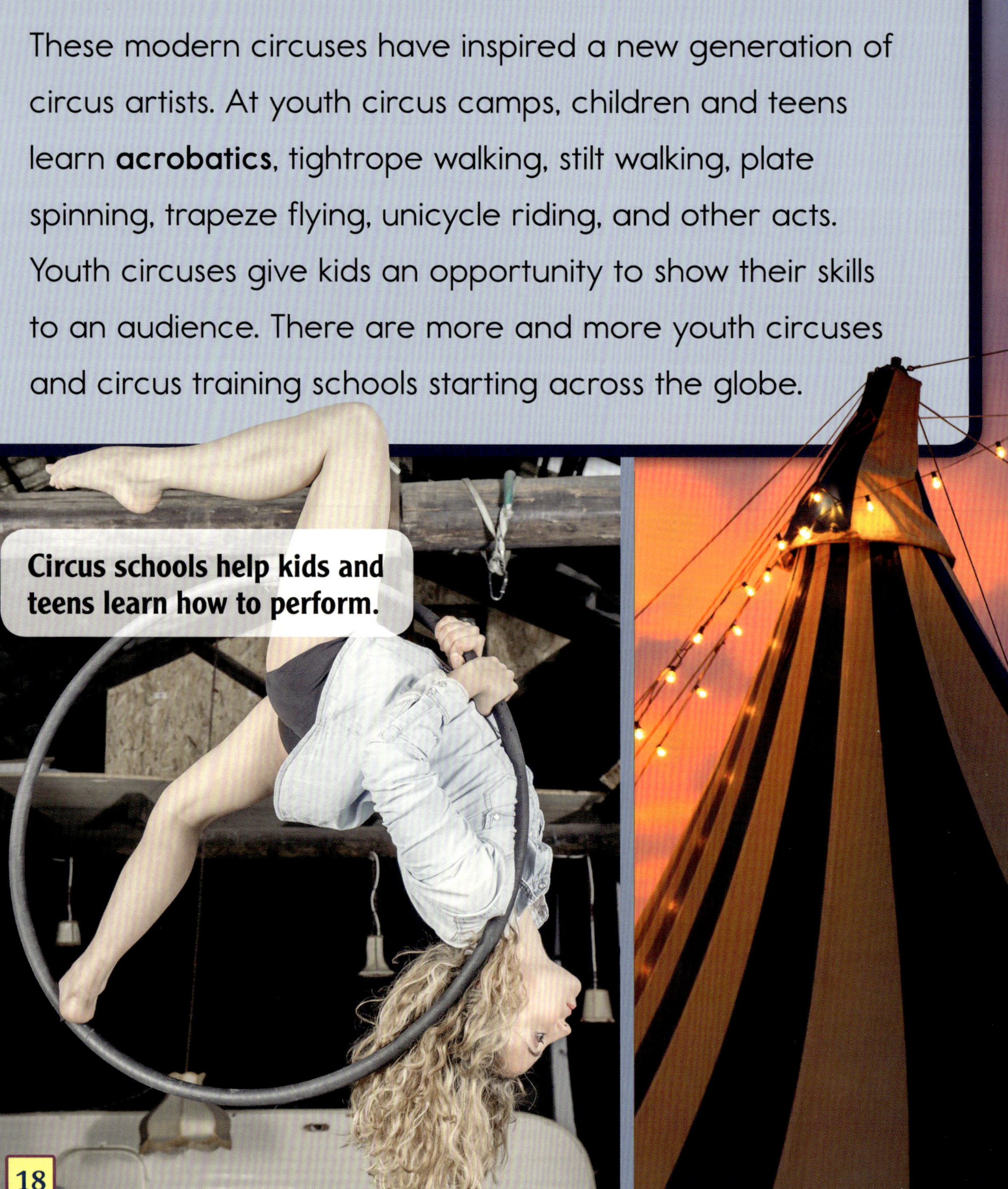

Circus schools help kids and teens learn how to perform.

The circus is one of the oldest shows on Earth. As long as people love the circus, the show will go on.

THE MODERN

2017
Ringling Bros. and Barnum & Bailey performs its final show

2017
Many nations and US states ban wild-animal acts in circuses

1984
Cirque du Soleil forms

1977
Big Apple Circus begins

1919
Ringling Bros. and Barnum & Bailey forms

TIMELINE OF CIR

1768
Circus begins in London, England

1793
First circus in the United States

1825
First use of tents

1872
P. T. Barnum starts his circus

1881
P. T. Barnum and James Bailey join together

1882
Barnum & Bailey Circus exhibits Jumbo the elephant

GLOSSARY

acrobatics
difficult or dangerous movements done by a performer

acrobats
people who perform gymnastic moves as part of a show

ancient
belonging to a time early in history

exotic
strange and unusual, or from a distant land

frontier
a distant area where few people live

legend
a story from the past that is believed by many people but cannot be proved

sanctuaries
safe places

troupe
a group of traveling performers

INDEX